PORTRAIT OF MY FATHER ·
IN AN ENGLISH LANDSCAPE

17.95

By the same author:

George Szirtes

Portrait of my Father
in an English Landscape

Oxford   New York

OXFORD UNIVERSITY PRESS

1998

Oxford University Press, Great Clarendon Street, Oxford OX2 6DP

Oxford New York

Athens Auckland Bangkok Bogota Bombay Buenos Aires
Calcutta Cape Town Dar es Salaam Delhi Florence Hong Kong Istanbul
Karachi Kuala Lumpur Madras Madrid Melbourne Mexico City
Nairobi Paris Singapore Taipei Tokyo Toronto Warsaw

and associated companies in
Berlin Ibadan

Oxford is a trade mark of Oxford University Press

First published in Oxford Poets
as an Oxford University Press paperback 1998

British Library Cataloguing in Publication Data

Data available

Library of Congress Cataloging in Publication Data
Szirtes, George, 1948–
Portrait of my father in an English landscape / George Szirtes.
p. cm. — (Oxford poets)
1. Fathers and sons—England—Poetry. 2. Hungarians—England—Poetry.
3. Sonnets, English. I. Title. II. Series.
PR6069.Z7P67 1998   821'.914—dc21   97–39070
ISBN 0-19-288091-8

1 3 5 7 9 10 8 6 4 2

Typeset by George Hammond Design
Printed in Great Britain by
Athenæum Press Ltd.
Gateshead, Tyne and Wear

ACKNOWLEDGEMENTS

Poems have appeared in *Ambit*, *Big Wide Words* (Poetry on the Buses), *Blade, Epoch* (USA), *The Hungarian Quarterly*, *London Magazine*, *Navis*, *New Writing 5*, *Poetry Wales*, *The Review* (USA), *The Rialto*, *The Richmond Review*, and the *Times Literary Supplement*.

A selection of the poems was broadcast on BBC Radio 3, as part of the programme 'Budapest 1956'. 'Portrait of my Father in an English Landscape' was broadcast as a programme on BBC Radio 3.

I am particularly grateful to the British Council for the opportunity of visiting Romania in the Spring of 1997.

The three long poems at the end of the book are in the form of a Hungarian Sonnet sequence, which consists of fifteen linked sonnets, where the last line of the first sonnet becomes the first of the second, and so forth, and the fifteenth sonnet is a sum of all the first lines. I have taken some minor liberties with the form.

G.S.

CONTENTS

Rabbits

The rabbits are about their business
of softening. They congregate in gangs
by hedgerows as if waiting for an event
of greater softness to overtake them.
The clouds overhead grow rabbit scuts
and bolt across the field in evening dress.
The whole sky is purpling with the scent
of evening. A clock opens and shuts
time out. Flowers bend on a single stem
and wind plumps leaves to wings.

Rabbits flicker into open spaces
all by themselves, exploratory, vague,
bristling in the wind, apologetic.
Out of sight, they settle
delicately then hop away, their faces
dreamy and purposive. They are a thick-
ening in the dark, a curl of soft metal,
a wholly benevolent plague
for which woolly words have to be invented,
something earth- and dropping- scented.

They lollop about in silence for a while,
shiver and bob, consume, dart back
into their holes, peek out. Soon the field
swallows them whole. The clock claps
its hands. They run off scared. The wind
bursts from a hedge and over a stile.
Leaves mumble, their lips are sealed.
The train swoops down its sinister track,
and the clouds make dramatic shapes
in the sky which is dropping like a blind.

Something of terror remains in the grass
where the rabbits have been. Night
comes on as the negative of daylight. Where
is the bristling gone? Something is shaking the train.
An old man holds his cup in trembling fingers,
waiting for the tremor to pass.
Insignificant stations swim through the air
in a fog of names. Some warmth lingers
in them and hovers there like a stain,
or a bird or a figure caught in mid flight.

Golden Bream

It may be nature morte *but it's still life*, said the joky sixties poet
and I'm sure he is right, because there is death in it,
not just in the codified clutter of skulls, books and bubbles
but in the whole enterprise and so particularly
when plainly dead creatures, like pheasants and hares,
quails, sparrows, orioles and trout (but chiefly the birds)

do so much lolloping and hanging, neatly shimmered up,
displayed with the instrument of their final bringing down,
and garnished with a few tasteful etceteras such as flowers,
and yes, they are beautiful, in every scale and feather,
and honest enough—they actually taste good
(those wonderful spices, the garlic, red onions,

the wine-water tinctures, the eggs, the pimentos and lemons)—
and despite what Berger says it's probably better
than owning the genuine things, somehow more touching
and dignified, almost transcendental, beyond material
through the material, a kind of sanctification
of the sensible world, moving in beatitudes,

with death in the centre (and what could be better?)
hovering tactfully beyond the sumptous canvas,
death with all its unlimited readings—a child in a fever,
the soldier in his trench, the burning villagers trapped
in a hut by the military, the grinding bastard that simply wears down
and exhausts you, all of which is in the nature of things

and you don't need to prove that, just look at these bream
who have clearly not survived nor ever could survive
the peninsular war or the hook, their furious
disappointed eyes telling you it's over, that the cold
has come too suddenly for even half-way reconciliation
between stillness on the one hand and life on the other.

Daffodils

I am bothered by the nagging translucency
of these daffodil petals in their Busby Berkeley outfits
of six yellow skirts around a frilled bell
darkening to its centre, their stern stalks bunched
in the glass on the sill by a warm brown wall,

and I'm wondering if I can make any sense of daffodils
(or Diaphenias or Daffy Ducks for that matter)
or of any of that unwonted clutter of names
which has done nothing to force them into flower
quite in the way they do here or to gather

those pleated petals to such concord of dancing
or stillness, recalling the skin of my mother
at fifty, slouched, puckered and dying,
her flame indrawn under bruised plums and purples,
or my skin, for instance, in its cold variations

on one theme of pink, full of cracking and byways
that grasp at the sunlight, almost transparent,
opening on something that passes them by
or cuts a swathe through them, not quite the sun,
but having the nonchalance of sunlight.

Mouth Music

i.m. Harold Woolhouse, botanist

Emma Kirkby is an expert on ethylene
we must get someone in to talk avocados
Burnham Beaches are down, the birds are protected
  said the dying man in gaunt profile on the bed

Così fan tutte is a fine work of fiction
one must hear the boom of the bittern, a bassoon would
probably do it, or a cello if it's cold
  said the dying man, his hands twittering twittering

Binsey Poplars with all its tall beeches is wailing,
the garden needs a good prune, a thorough dactylic,
the sumach has pinnate leaves much like a rabbit
  said the dying man, his head battered and fossilised

But we love him, said the visitors, and his words are disturbing
the bastions are down, all the high scaffolding down
the language is folding in on itself, fold down the covers
  said the dying man in his pride and withering

Between words grow the senses one hears in the night-time
or smells in the daytime, that lodge in one's tonsils
like airy cabbages or clouds full of antonyms
  said the dying man to the living in his wisdom

But we want him here with us, just as he has been
just as we hope that we ourselves will be, where the wind
sings in the attic and the water seeps through the stones in the cellar
  here where we sit and make noises of talking

The noises of talking, a botanical opera, the sound of a number
on the way to becoming, all this amounts to a kind
of affection which has its own logic, the visitors protested
  as the dead man lay talking and the furniture listened

as furniture must by its nature having no tongue
to tell of its sorrows, having no lexicon, language or logic
and incapable of becoming by simply changing position
        by booming or bawling or bursting into childish tears.

Man with a Surgical Collar,
Woman Encumbered with Kindness

1

He sits in his armchair wearing his plain ruff.
She appears through the hatch like a face
on television. Time is peculiar stuff
and moves at its own under-rated pace.

2

He is remembering China and Hertfordshire. He writes
as he thinks and every so often a soft sharp
burst of laughter explodes and all China ignites
and tinkles like light on a rusting wind harp.

3

She is reading poetry. The language is playing
her as it might a piano. What can it draw
from those strings and hammers? Notes are straying
into chords, their harmonies sweet and raw.

4

She calls on the sick woman down the street
before she knows she's sick. The uninsured
may not be covered but kindness has soft feet
to tiptoe on, and soon the sick are cured.

5

He crooks his little finger. His grandson crooks
his own and they shake fingers. This is normal.
Such modes of greeting survive in secret books
reserved for connoisseurs who like things formal.

Gunsmith

All day the gas-jet glows in the gunsmith's window.
His long slow face is yellow with it. He smiles
like a shy man, even his moustache is shy.
Plainly he loves his work, he takes so much care with it.

Chiefly it's polishing, soothing, easing the barrel clean,
rubbing down abrasions, filing out a scratch,
straightening sights. He is making an object,
himself a part of the product of his skill.

Thoroughly gentle, almost apologetic,
how difficult it would be to dislike him
in his honest endeavour, his modest demeanour

as he turns the barrel over, blows hot dust away,
as he makes space for himself in the glow of his window,
in the soft detonations of light when somebody enters.

Tinseltown

Nothing but a glittering you can't describe,
nothing but names and smiling at faces: no
jewels but plastic beads, no tiaras but card,
no face but that which fits you, a tall mirror
hung by the magazine rack, some pearls of frost
on the window beyond, dripping elegance,

full of December, and rain starting to dance
on the pavement where a woman has just crossed
this busy road to push through the double door
to where you stand by the counter, working hard,
totting money at the till in a green glow
of figures, servant to that commonplace tribe

queuing for papers though it's nothing to do
with you what the tabloids blaze across the front
page, you simply read it along with the rest
and it's good for a giggle, just like this crown
of tinsel you got wound into your hair, which
catches the lampglow all the way down the aisle

and slips occasionally forward, so while
you are counting you're always having to switch
hands and flick the thing back so it won't fall down,
but sits perky and sparkling, a silver nest
of light, frivolous, and when it falls you don't
stop to pick it up, it means nothing to you.

The First, Second, Third and Fourth Circles

I

Most cities approximate to a circle and so does this,
curled about the double bend of its river, on one side snuggling
to cliffs and hills where the cool air shuffles through a park with cedars,
a cog-wheeled railway, a deserted tram stop,
some concrete tables for ping-pong or for chess,
and benches where migrant workers from Romania
sleep to shave in the morning by a working fountain,
hearing at night the wind in its mild cups
stumble up stairs between gardens, trailing a cloak
of lightbulbs and shopsigns over the gentler slopes
which are peopled with villas and baroque excrescences,
belvederes, weathervanes, cherubs and furies, cupolas and turrets,
a wrought-iron gate with doorbells and nameplates
which allows a visiting wind to drift through the hallway
between two apartments whose front doors give on to
large Ottoman carpets and rugs hung on walls,
and endless shelves of once-subsidized literature,
to say nothing of rattling East German spin-driers,
expressionist plumbing and between-the-wars pictures
such as are found even in bedrooms of fifties estates
where no one's disturbed except for the sheepdog
slumped on a doormat, listening to its owners
snoring aloud in partitioned compartments
stuffed with old furniture intended for bigger rooms,
or howling to late cars or the crumbling glass
shattered on the high street where two drunks are fighting
and the police pick up girls from discos just for the hell of it,
doing handbrake turns by domed turkish baths
sweeping down the embankment, past the olympic pool,
the chain-store installed in a reconditioned cellar,
the emptying restaurant with tables in the yard
where a few stray napkins float between chairlegs
in this mildest of weathers down in the square
or up at the museum-palace with its soaring prospects
and prancing statues of princes pulling faces
at the black of the night-time Danube, surveying the far side.

2

Cars are creeping round the portico of the Prussian style Academy,
the Westminster gothic of Parliament and the fifties modernist
White House of what was just a few years ago
the party headquarters, and beyond it the boulevard,
Angelfield, New Pest, and the distant industrial suburbs
beyond the third of the ring roads, the third arc shielding the second,
and the second haunting the contours of old city walls
embedded in tenements of the innermost ring,
pierced by radial highways, cafés, department stores.

3

Nineteenth-century grid-maps where everyone lives
but wants to move out of, in one room or two rooms
or one and a half-rooms, ranged about the communal courtyard,
the sound of a tap or a radio, a beggar or busker,
under the residents' own square of sky, towards which climb
neglected stairs with blown-away putti,
untrustworthy lift-shafts which back in the dark days
brought terror to everyone, when in the dawn hours
the lift started up and a car was seen at the entrance,
and a single shepherded figure disappeared off the grid-map
into uncharted country beyond the reach of the suburbs.

4

The local girls are offering rides in a handy apartment
to the accompaniment perhaps of a video,
while next door, behind secessionist doors,
the lecturer types out his lecture and the German quiz host
slides down a cable which the whole block has paid for
and a lost voice interrogates itself at the mirror
or sips from its little black cup of resentments
which keep the heart beating all through the night.

The House Stripped Bare By Her Bachelors, Even

The outer layers are gone. The houses shiver
in brick underwear. They feel the shame of it.
Their iron bones embarrass them. The river
has worn them down and left them bare,
all edges and splinter, wispy as maidenhair.

They are softer than they think. Fingers of lead
have probed their sides, shells dug them in the ribs.
Friable earth, they crumble into gutters,
shower with white dust the blind head
of the man in the doorway, wave broken shutters
at each other like so many soiled bibs.

The bachelors who stripped them bare are blowing
about the street with sweetpapers and other ephemera,
seedy old raincoats lost in a dust haze,
who hesitate, vaguely aware of where they are going
humming an air from a pre-war opera,
if only they could think of the name of it.

The Idea of Order at the József Attila Estate

The lawns are in order, someone is keeping them neat.
No one has yet tipped rubbish down from the tenth floor.
People are walking their dogs or waiting for buses
As if they had taken to heart the architect's fiction of order,
And saw their own lives in exploded and bird's eye views.

It all has an explanation. The woman once sentenced to death,
The silver beard of the courier-spy, the pentathlete,
The shrunken delicacy of the woman with the zimmer frame.
These lives fit together as if in a programme, a drawing
In a department, one all-embracing stroke of genius.

The lifts rise like zips. They do up the block which maintains
The sealed and communal weather of its residents.
It is peaceful and calm in their versions of being
A dream of files and cabinets at uniform temperature
Where death entails merely a comfortless distancing,

Something diffuse, clouds seen from the roof garden,
Thousands of breathing cells misting up windows,
Waste materials flushed down arterial pipeways,
The voices of children scrambling upstairs,
And the distant suburban railway coming and going.

The Manchurian Candidate

Imagine your own thoughts are not your own,
that you're a puppet waiting for a sign,
some secret signal, which will set you off
down pre-ordained paths along a narrow line
unrecognizable to you, a way unknown
except within your nerves. This is the stuff
of nightmares, and your Laurence Harvey face
stares strenuously back half out of place.

Imagine a small town in the Midwest:
one day you are confronted by a mass
of slimy matter, a blob that comes and eats
folk's innards out and monstrously can pass
through windows, walls and doors. Perhaps it's best
not to think of this. And soon the thing retreats
into its hidden spacecraft, disappears
for months at a time, or even a few years.

Imagine a place, a clean white house, some chairs
set out on porches. This place belongs to you.
It's like a mind, fresh-washed, hung out to dry.
It smells of comfort, offers a fine view
of lawns and streets the whole neighbourhood shares.
Somewhere a neighbour's child begins to cry,
a radio blares, or you hear a woman shout,
then rain comes down to wash the memory out.

Variations on Radnóti: Postcards 1989

1

A wicked cherub perched on a pilaster
(His torso only) portending disaster
In somebody's gateway.
He grins and winks: half menace, half play.

2

The bustiest blonde in town some six yards high
who smirks behind sunglasses on a fire-wall
advertising the state lottery, may be a spy
but is in any case far from impartial.
If only I could squeeze her mammoth four-foot tits
I too might manage on state benefits.

3

Mother and child on a balcony,
Behind them the river stirs and shifts.
Parliament looks on and creaks
Down delicate buttresses and broken lifts.

4

The miracle of the statue's foot which leaks
medicinal water. The miracle of the boutiques.
The miracle of wirtschaftswunder. But now we are
Talking one miracle too far.

5

This is more like it, a balding middle-aged man
feet firmly planted, a mild pot belly, dressed
in quasi-military gear;
in his hand a peaked cap and a thirty-year plan
to confound both east and west,
give or take a year.

Busby Berkeley in the Soviet Union

I

It's the Ministry of Culture Symphony Orchestra,
a sly and dangerous band of men
living in Stalin's greatcoat, with Dmitri
Shostakovich jammed into one pocket, Beria
into another. Distant echoes of glittery
ballrooms and a harvest moon

where a silent snake of Conga dancers grinds out figures-
of-eight to routines impeccably
transferred from Berkeley in true Soviet spirit—
sinister choruslines consisting of beggars
and blondes in collusion, employed by the KGB.
Together yet separate

in each square of space, they spin to light froth, coagulate
to stiff geometries, symbolic
of the will of the party and people. With set
expressions of joy they're working to liquidate
whatever is louche, undisciplined or chaotic.
Forests of arms and legs float

on crystalline marble. They're playing a waltz in the pit,
terpsichorean labourers, miners
of melody, glossy anonymous ranks
of Stakhanovites, brigades of polish and spit.
Light, anaesthetic, sexy, a row of binliners
in satin rises and sinks.

The girls flash thighs and high pale knickers, ingratiating
and threatening at once. We dance on
brittle but enchanted legs. The nightmare years
are back, more seductive than ever, aching,
lyrical. Outside, undesirables have begun
to gather. The walls have ears.

2

This music is in your blood, slithering through your arteries.
It's no longer 1934
but whatever you want. Call it today if
it pleases you. You're watching TV, some series
about hospitals or cops, an investigator
on the scent or a plaintiff

in a court case or a documentary about fish,
it doesn't matter what kind of tripe
you fancy, you get it all, good quality.
So you think you are safe, but under the rubbish
it raises its head. Sweet music. Suddenly you wipe
your face. Electricity

courses through you, or is it nostalgia? Insidious
and creepy, you hear it mount the stair
like desire. It makes you feel horny, childlike,
delighted. It's like going out to the pictures
on a rainy night when water catches in your hair
and the yellow streetlights strike

along the puddles. You shut your eyes and see regiments
of soldiers or dancers shuffling by
and know they're beckoning for you to join them.
The glamour's irresistible, the sounds and scents
of the crowd, you're taking your part in a tragedy
or marching to an anthem

drunk yet disciplined, Dionysiac, in the triumph
of your will or somebody else's,
the people's, the state's, the zeitgeist's, direct
and certain, carried along in the mighty oomph
of the band as it marches past familiar houses,
impeccable, bright, correct.

Four Villonesques on Desire

Some can only lust for what is gone, for the grey
in the green. There are those for whom beauties in their graves
exude a legendary perfume in which they can play
out their mortality. Some sing about desire in waves
of the sea, desire at the all-night raves
of the energetic young, desire in the emptiness
of mid-morning, desire in warm salty caves.
The well-dressed body, they say, needs sometimes to undress.

There are those, they sing, who cannot drive demons away
however they try. Men who prefer close shaves.
Women who itch, people who spend the whole day
dreaming of what their imagination craves,
those who are bastards, nasty vicious slaves
to hurt. Those who fall victim to a light caress.
Those who long for crucifixions under classical architraves.
The well-dressed body, they say, needs sometimes to undress.

Some cannot help but touch themselves. Some pray
for deliverance. Some, so the song goes, believe that lust depraves.
Some kill. Some die. Some prefer to frequent gay
clubs, some want to dance down church naves
in the nude. Some sit around in pious conclaves
condemning themselves. Some look an awful mess.
Some paint themselves up like Indian braves.
The well-dressed body, they say, needs sometimes to undress.

Think of all those Jims and Jos and Sals and Dis and Daves
whose numbers are constant and will never grow less.
God knows how the mind seized by desire behaves.
The well-dressed body, it says, needs sometimes to undress.

Where are the snows and the beautiful wanton
women? Venetia Digby for example, whose bust
John Aubrey saw in a brasier's window, or Anne
Herbert, Duchess of Pembroke? Salacious dust.
Where's Mistress Overall, married to the Mast-
er of Catherine Hall and he much horned by her
but faithful to her beauty, unto the last.
In what air does their sweet dust stir?

Dear dead women with such hair . . . Venetian
broad-bosomed dames, objects of a poet's lust—
less lust than desire at best and not for anyone
in particular—flighty girls no one could trust
with a few glasses in them if a lover would but persist.
The Crazy Janes, Wild Alices, all flying fur
and impulse, who should have been gagged and trussed.
In what air does their sweet dust stir?

Have horses bolted? Have they fired a gun?
What have they sniffed or drunk or thrust
into their hungry mouths? Did they lie in the sun
too long? Have they woken the collective disgust
of Tunbridge Wells or finally earned that honest crust?
Did they roll in the grass, the moon a blur
of light, their eyes half closed, faintly nonplussed?
In what air does their sweet dust stir?

Has all their fine metal turned to a mournful rust?
Could danger or duty or discovery deter
them from their pleasures or did they do as they must?
In what air does their sweet dust stir?

3 THE SELFISH GENE

Where are they gone? Where are their atomies
swirling now? Where are those selves that meant
them and them only? Are they swarming like bees
in the garden waiting for an appropriate event,
or are they like ghostly soldiers in a ghostly tent
somewhere in the fields? Where is the queen
of bedroom and headroom with her exquisite scent?
What has become of the selfish gene?

Desire is a breaking apart, a great orgasmic sneeze
of pollen and dust, with no one competent
to reassemble what is lost. Where are Claire's knees?
Lolita's teenage American limbs? Girls who leant
from windows as the parade passed, the disobedient
daughters of parents who tried to intervene
in their affairs but were forced to admit themselves impotent?
What has become of the selfish gene?

What can you do once the miraculous geometries
of spirit or being are shattered? Whatever patience went
to their making, they are now blown on the breeze
which tickles other people's fancies. Kate's innocent
look was perfected over years. No one can reinvent
her curl of lip, nor Jenny's starved and epicene
quiver, her brown eyes wide, all energy spent . . .
What has become of the selfish gene?

All of them proper subjects for lament,
if only there were not so much hot air in between.
What was essence and what was embellishment?
What has become of the selfish gene?

Where is May Trevithick, sender of short rhymes
and collector of articles on the uses of urine? Where
is intimidating Susan with her list of crimes
against the imagination? Where is the spare
Elisabeth, drugged and heartstopped, with her black hair
and soft voice? Where is John McClure,
drowned in a French river, drunk on vin ordinaire?
Do pheromones die with the spoor?

Where's Derek Whiteley with his seed-times
and old roses, his institutions and professor's chair?
Where is his seed now? Where are the lost primes
of Tim the ace-guitarist and Alan Jarvis, the fair-
haired beautiful lodger? In whose tender care
is Martin Bell who finished up almost sober but poor
with his Desnos, Reverdy and Anne Hébert?
Do pheromones die with the spoor?

Where are the illustrious dead with their Guggenheims
and Pulitzers? Did they enjoy their due share
of fame and desire? Is death sexy? What agent limes
the twig their spirits are caught on when brightness falls from the air?
Beside the Deans, the Marilyns and Judys is there
a myth capacious enough to accommodate the glamour
we ourselves knew, once so close, in the bed, at the foot of the stair?
Do pheromones die with the spoor?

Where are the ones we forget, whose absence we bear
with equanimity, simply because they're not here anymore,
and we have to? Who carry our longings unaware?
Do pheromones die with the spoor?

Whispers

What the old whisper to the young
which makes their hair stand on end
is what would never be told
by lover or friend

What the old ones shrouded and scarved
do with their hands and lips
is a secret they breathe through teeth
and fingertips

What beautiful muscles the young
exhibit to the old
What wonderful curves of rump
to stroke or scold

But it's secret, it's secret, a sin
to reveal except in air,
old fingers crumpled as clothes
the young won't wear

Porcupine

When the porcupine seductress
and the fat executive
sail away to happiness
and all the fish forgive

the net in which they're caught,
the hook that slits their throat
and little mermaids sport
like dolphins round the boat,

when love grows ears and fingers
and snouts incline to kiss,
and songs require no singers
then let them sing you this

let them sing their pleasure
let them sing their night,
the executive's fat treasure,
the porcupine's delight

Cat in the Bag

Always the whispering
Always the doubt
To keep the cat in
Or let the cat out

It's a dark old country
Riddled with heresy
Torturers, murderers
All in conspiracy,

Nothing you say
Will settle their hash
You stoke up the fire
They send down the ash

What earthly use
Are the mountains of dollars
And those brilliant cruel
Carnival colours

Whatever you do
Cats stay in their bags
The rich in their villas
The poor in their rags

The poor in their rags
The dogs at their vomit
What earthly good
Can ever come of it

Directing an Edward Hopper

Life is like this, only more so,
life being what life was and was dreamt to be
to music in the cinematic glow
of streetlights, a barman stirring a daiquiri,

a plate-glass window, the wind cautious,
raising my hair above the railtrack
where a train is expected and rushes
below, tugging purple shadows at its back,

a reassuring sinister sense of the dark
warehouse at the back of the mind,
the boredom of the bench in the park,
and those extraordinary blind

silences we collapse into on hot days
where all we want is to shut our eyes
and stretch out on the bed in a blaze
of floral wallpaper, while the suitcase lies

at our feet and we are half packed,
ready to go, as if the script
of our lives demanded it, our soundtracked
conversation tightly gripped

in the safe hands of the future
which is pure nostalgia. That is where
I am headed now, that miniature
version of our elsewhere,

and when we love we shall look as dated
as imagined childhood,
a childhood I myself have created
and would escape from if I could.

Day of the Dead, Budapest

Down the main arterials, on ring roads, in alleyways,
The dead stand perpendicular with heads ablaze.
And some of them blow out, while others burn right down
And leave small patches of darkness like footsteps about town

Sap Green: Old School

The copper dome of the old school had turned
into the colour of soup they used to serve
on certain Fridays. The dining-hall lights burned,
low in the autumn gloom. You boys deserve

all you get, muttered the head into his gown.
A desperate smell of tobacco. The old man
had a bad smoker's cough, his fingers brown
with age and decay, faintly reptilian.

Retreating backwards into the fog, the class
of '65 were entering the pool
of memory through dark translucent glass
the colour of sap. It was time's own school,

uniforms languishing in cloakroom showers;
the loss, the charm of wasted after hours.

Prussian Blue: Dead Planets

The dead planets have gathered a deposit
of Prussian blue. The moonlight leaves them cold,
the sun has moved to other regions, their old
friends have deserted them. They are content to sit

in their dust, while under the dust, a mild ash
is still cooling and will go on cooling for aeons.
Out at midnight, children observe millions
of dead stars or watch a passing aeroplane flash

its wingtips at them. There is music in space,
a deep thrumming between plane and cello
that settles in the stomach and helps the digestion,

a pulpy, smooth, emollient interface.
It is absolute, abides no question.
It sings to crimson lake and lemon yellow.

Sometimes, under a tired eye, you see
the faintest ring of Prussian blue and think
how sad it is, like the faded ink
of a dead uncle's letter or the shadow of a tree

or a peasant's skirt, and you wonder what
it's doing there, under the eyes. Can one believe
in beauty like some simpleton and leave
the rest to sort itself out, rely on the gut

with its weakness for violins and sentimental songs?
The very idea is absurd. But listen! Do you hear them?
Bells! Bells across the street. Deep Prussian souls

muttering to puddles and cars. The world belongs
to perceptions of the world. The mice in their holes
creep out to sniff the cats but don't go near them.

Chalk White: The Moon in the Pool

for Clarissa

1

Between classical columns the water lies
rippling its faint skin to the sexy moon.
Breast fills with milk, eyes roll and weep, wind tries
to creep between damp petals. Dawn soon.
Between time. Not sleep but a kind of dull
zombie wakefulness. I float like a ghost,
knocking against the hard walls of my skull,
uncomfortable, dissatisfied and lost.
You breathe. Breathe and rise. Mumble. Stir. Hover
in the darkness that is on the point of breaking.
Your flesh is sweet warm dough under the cover.
Light begins to slide over you, aching
with a kind of passion. It speaks. My dear,
it says, its voice unexpectedly near.

2

My dear, says the moon, says the water, say
the classical columns. Their tenderness
surprises me. It is not like them to display
such human frailty. They usually dress
like dandies or symbols. In any case
there are no columns, no moon, only sounds
made by words whispering, a mouth, a face,
lack and desire, language doing its rounds.
O, says the moon and nothing more. And O
replies its reflection in the dark pool
under the eyes. What else makes such a glow
in the night, or echoes through the locked school
where we learned to love each other and talk
about love, diagrams drawn in moon-chalk?

3

Let's bring it down to real time. Almost three
in the morning early in the new year.
I've been awake an hour, can faintly see
your hair, could easily whisper in your ear.
But you were tired last night. I move with care
as I search for clothes. The word 'beautiful'
comes to me as I look at you. And you are
beautiful. It is as if a bowl full
of water were carefully balanced on a tray
and I were carrying it through the closed door,
desperate not to spill it. And a ray
of what could only be called moonlight or
felt like moonlight touched it and the door
opened into the hall with its cold moonlit floor.

4

Try again. I want to make the moonlight
vanish. I want to hold your face without
its glamorous appurtenances, to write
the moon without anything to write about
except the weight of your face in my hands
which has a meaning I will not have made,
which language itself broadly understands,
which is what you too would see if you stayed
in the white noise of the mirror, or ran
into a dream full tilt to emerge whole
and awake. But I am only a man
whose presence prefers to call itself a soul,
and you are asleep, and there's no moon
except this one in the pool and soon it is gone.

Cerulean Blue: Footnote on Wim Wenders

Angels do exist. Wim Wenders almost
had them right with that slightly shop-soiled look,
neither pure spirit, nor pure intellect, lost
on some level of their own, their eyes in a book

but raised fatally in a cool engagement,
and there they hold you and you feel looked through
but with a vague and troubling presentiment
at the colour, somewhere between grey and blue

intensifying to clear sky which is
merely a form of seduction, and you sigh,
already smitten, and get on with your business

which is what it always was. You start to count
the coins in your pocket or the spots on someone's tie
but keep losing track of the amount.

Just as, for example, you might sit down
at a table and begin to swim in pale smoke.
The sun floats in the window. Whole years drown
in your coffee and you start to remember a joke

without a punch line when an angel rises
from your companion's mouth and calmly hovers
above her head but your self-possession surprises
even you, and the thought of becoming lovers

solidifies like a screen on which is projected
the dream-film of all those other lives which are
not yours, and before you know, you've interjected

some ambiguous remark the angel hears
and sniggers at, then moves off to the bar
with his transparent head and disappears.

Romanian Brown

for Irina Horea

Political crises, shortages, rising crime.
The dictator's palace is unwittingly postmodern.
Life proceeds under the now-benign, now-stern
paternal gaze of Freudian Father Time.

If looks could kill . . . In high-rise flats the click
of keyboards. The gentle sea-sigh of computers:
fingertips of neighbouring literatures
touch across the corpse of the body politic.

Editors and translators conspire in the cold.
A chill runs down those delicate hands.
The TV spouts videos, foreign rock bands:
nothing now can ever again grow old.

Beggars are drifting through deserted squares
like paper sacks or ghosts of dancing bears.

Under the eyes a deep raw umber opens
into the warmth of the self like a letting-go,
and one slides through it to the marrow
in the thigh-bone and the thick translucent lens

of the joints. It is as strange as the world;
as disturbing in its brilliant intimacy
as the metaphor of the heart, that literary
device; as odd as the drowned sailor's pearled

and erotic eyes; as peculiar as the voice
you hear when you speak. No one who lives
in ordinary rooms with the great imperatives
of work and need lives there entirely by choice.

To sit in the dark settees of the eye is to know
the heart as literature, to suffer and let go.

Warm greys and browns. The softer certainties
assume jumpers and skirts, melt into tights.
The world must be civilized. Each colour invites
a cool intimacy between intelligent entities.

Long spatulate fingers stretch across a web
of nerves cocooning the fly of desire
which must nourish us somehow. But we tire
of its endless demands and night too starts to ebb.

The night is dark as coffee. The bushes outside
move in the wind, both hot and cold at once.
The trees are tossing their heads with impatience
and the whole sky begins suddenly to slide.

A kind of desperation runs through the deep
brown of the eyes and judders into sleep.

Solitary climbers sleeping at the tense
edge of precipitous forests under a dark brown
shower of needles stolidly arrowing down
into the earth can feel a bear's presence

(there are still bears in Europe, and wolves too)
in the soft pad and roll of the wind as it treads
towards them. The early autumn sheds
furred leaves which gradually form a thick glue

and a bird sings on the sharp snow-covered peak.
A woman lies in her tent, her dark brown hair
spread beneath her like the claws of a bear,
and all the bears and wolves begin to speak.

In a clear glass of Irish whisky a train
pulls away from the platform through dawn rain.

A deep smudge of brown, something like a forest,
suggests an entrance into a possible past.
The dead come and go there like the forgotten caste
of an old religion. A woman offers her breast

to someone frail or a wolf or some kind of bird
in a potent act of charity or witchcraft.
The leaves are shivering in a delicate draught
between the pages of a book, hidden under a word.

Someone is saying: *Nature is your mother
and father* and points to a hole in the ground.
Lips meet lips with a distant sucking sound
and the hair rises, soft as a pigeon's feather.

Magic is suspect. An ancient figure stumps
between two sets of rusted petrol pumps.

The cloacal anteroom of the railway station. Pale
urinal yellows of the early morning.
The whole country disappears without warning
swallowed by night. The dark begins to fail.

But to think, and think . . . and now thin lines of steam
creep through the compartment, unfurl in grey,
briefly compose themselves before fading away.
The trains are coupling in a wet dream.

The bears are here too. They lumber across the track
in their furred overcoats. I watch them sadly.
I put out my hand to them. I know how badly
I need them. And look, they are calling me back.

And then I drift awake. And soon we start.
The train shakes like a tremor in the heart.

Blown like faint dust into the universe
whose eyes are both distant and close, this nagging pain
accompanies the sensation of being home again
as if one's own life were running in reverse.

Backwards into youth, backwards into childhood, back
into something formless yet vital, a directionless force
that stirs and disturbs. Somewhere a rocking horse
rises and dips, mouth grimaces then grows slack,

relaxing into a satisfied droop of the lips.
It doesn't last. The dust is whirling up a storm
desperate for affection, the remembered form
of the reaching hand as it grasps the bar and grips.

Raw umber, the rawer the better. The wood
receives you with its unfathomable good.

Lemon Yellow: A Twist of Lemon

for WSU, 3 May 1997

Nothing so bitter yet fresh as this small sun
radiating in a glass of clear liquid, be it
water or gin, fizzy or still. You see it
hanging there, doing no harm to anyone

till it hits home, when the face begins to slew
into a mask of hate, almost Japanese
in its exertions, then by subtle degrees
settle back into repose, a residue

of sunlight turning green at the gills, just there
at the tip of the nose, or in the fine
hairs on the neck, impossible to define,
soon vanishing away into thin air.

And all the bitterness is gone, discreet
as a trusted friend, and everything tastes sweet.

So one forgives everything, even time
whose bitter pill is harder to digest.
So one forgives the wormwood at the breast
which might yield milk, and the sublime

gall of indifference which drips unconcerned
from early morning trees. And one forgives
the tiny miseries and petty purgatives
one has to swallow, all that one has learned

and unlearned only to have to learn again,
the grating words, sullen as lemon rind,
with which the ungenerous reward the kind
whose anger fades after a count of ten.

Some like to suck the lemon, slice by slice
and let it slip into their hearts like ice.

How delicious the lemon is. It cools
the eye and settles at the back of the throat.
You shudder at its touch, at its remote
acidic laughter and its spiky molecules.

If hell is like lemons, one could get used to it.
In the vestibule café waiters like demons
proffer a trident stuck with bitter lemons
each slice so sticky the tongue gets fused to it.

But even here forgiveness wins the day
anticipating the sweetness that is sure
to follow something so stinging and so pure.
Sweetness will come: there's just a short delay.

And that wonderful light, concentrated, tense
in its yellow vest, proclaims its immanence.

The sponge soaked in vinegar. The feet
bunched like keys. The fingers bent and splayed.
The ragged children running in the shade
to a hot drum. The inescapable beat

of blood in the ear. Bitter, bitter. The quick
skip and twitch of the heart. You imagine
it all like drowning in pure oxygen
as the air begins to harden and grow thick.

Now the delicate tendons in your wrist
begin to ache and tears well up like drops
of the purest poison. And then the pain stops,
disappears suddenly, almost unnoticed.

The sun, bright as a lemon, sweet and calm,
trickles like sweat into your open palm.

Flesh Pink: The Face in the Coat

for Helen at twenty-one

The world is full of faces. Folded behind their eyes
faces travel to work, arrive in fields, before
a whirring camera, and briefly summarize
their wisdom and desires. Where can we store
all their knowledge? On some machine with a reel
of film inside it? Such beautiful expressions
in full face or in profile are tempting to steal
or steal from, to plagiarize their confessions
and their gorgeous landscapes. Even on trains,
they leave a brief powder that fills your throat,
emanations of inwardness, faint stains
on seats where they once slumped like a discarded coat.
Hold on to its tails. We are of the same stuff
as travelled there. You never know enough.

Time is boredom. Children in the paper say
they are bored. They are moving at the speed
of light, which is not as it was in their teachers' day,
but faster, ever faster, till all the long days bleed
one into another, each an eternity
without dimension. Now you see it, now
you don't. Childish tedium has no pity.
Perhaps it is not to be relieved, not anyhow.
Later the process changes, though not for a while
and not so as you'd notice. The policeman
quotes Dante, the shepherd dreams, girls smile
at the camera. It is, as they say, all in the can.
The bored child is forever bored. The kiss is frozen.
Soft mouths everywhere, soft mouths by the dozen.

The cliché about the camera stealing your soul
is perfectly true. Someone must possess it—
a relative, a friend, strangers at a market stall.
The soul is photogenic: how to address it?
To have held a small face in your hands
is to guess its nature. You watch it grow, but what
it becomes is something no one understands.
Time excels at the editorial cut,
likes journeys and films or any kind of sequence,
but loses the plot and has to improvise,
and what it completes need not make too much sense
as long as it provides minimal food for the eyes.
Everyone is a star, for more than fifteen minutes,
more than enough to fill the short half-life of sonnets.

The Looking-Glass Dictionary

for Gabriel Fitzmaurice

1

Words withheld. Words loosed in angry swarms.
An otherness. The whole universe was
other, a sum of indeterminate forms
in motion. Who knows what the neighbour does
behind closed doors? You hear the chime
of the doorbell, the faint mechanical
music of the radio. It's supper time.
A window opens on a cry or chuckle,
the rest is half withheld—should it be loosed
the window's quickly shut, the door slammed tight
to seal words in. Guessed at or deduced
darkness arrives feathering words with night.
There they grow wings, like owls and nightingales,
screeching or singing till their meaning stales.

2

Screeching or singing till its meaning stales,
the cold grey light has drawn you from your bed,
the words go scuttling homeward, their bright tails
between their legs and shelter in your head.
The airport. Night. December. Rough and grey,
a blanket covers you. The windows snore
half-way between dust and snow. The day,
trying to raise itself, creeps under the door
and offers you a cup of tea. Its alien milk
enters your bloodstream like the wizened face
of the old woman with her tray. That silk
ribbon of liquid confirms your sense of place,
and winds you in, a line that anchors, warms,
and lets you enter its own world of forms.

3

They let you enter their strange world of forms
out in the playground, on the rough brick wall
where they have left their messages in storms
of chalk and paint. Their distances still call
for you, back in the classroom or a street
at some resort where you once spent the summer
among arcades, to the rock and roll beat
of neon lights, and further out and dimmer,
a buoy blinking through foggy yellow air
or the gentle drone of cricket commentary
in daytime heat which wraps you in blonde hair
and scent of oil, that dies in memory,
hovering in a haze before it fails,
like faint vibrations down deserted rails.

4

Faint vibrations of trains along the rails:
where are we now? Abroad again or home?
Between two kinds of sound. Their echo trails
along behind you (words themselves won't come).
What did your mother say before you woke
to this? Her ribs vibrated with the thrum
of inner traffic. Something like a croak
surfaced at your throat and the hot drum
of her heartbeat made your heart dance. The slow
pulse of her blood blubbed and retreated, drove
your tongue before it with its enormous O,
and educated you to the word 'love'.
Like all words that apply and predicate
desire and loss, it brooked of no debate.

5

Desire and loss do not permit debate.
Where do the inner journeys go? They end
in trails of words, a kind of nonsense state
you cannot trust. And true, it is no friend
to kindness or reason. Words were treacherous.
Do you remember how at school they made
you catch the worms you would dissect? The fuss
as they wriggled and stiffened in formaldehyde?
The Latin names that crystallized that weak
mulch of muscle? The humours of the eye
that wept and spurted a transparent streak
of laughter between a language and a cry?
The Queen's English wrapped the pain in sound
that was articulate, in which the pain was drowned.

6

Articulate, you know how pain is drowned
and resurrected, undergoes baptism
and dies once more. The vessel runs aground
time and time again, drawn to the bosom
that nourished it. First time I saw the sea
was in December at Westgate. Huge grey jaws
snapped at the rocks, the white seethed in fury
like a pan full of fat, but cold. One word draws
the sea up, another repels it. We met
in a hut on the cliff top, cub scouts with string
and diagrams of knots. The faint sun set
on the horizon. We were children playing
with water pistols. Food appeared on the plate
like clockwork and the clock did not run late.

7

But clockwork sometimes runs down or runs late.
The words my mother spoke were rarely home
to her, or moved at another, slower rate
which could not follow her. Somehow the room
was never hers. When she was cross, her eyes
ran before language, even before her voice,
which issued from a deep, raw, oversize
mouth inside her. We knew she had no choice,
that it would be all kindness, kisses, tears.
After the terrors (the camp, the deaths, the strange
sexual crudeness) we knew that what appears
is merely a sign and yields life little change,
that mum was a sea that ran your ship aground,
her voice a channel for that kind of sound.

8

A narrow channel. Now the empty sound
of a ship's engine, now a soft gull peeling
from the clouds, a bruise or an old wound,
plaster cracked across the bedroom ceiling.
The ceiling rose opens in a brilliant blur
and the bulb in the rose expands in purple
echoes of itself. The rain is damp fur
on the window. Your bedclothes ripple
in the night tide as you swim the sudden dark.
Your parents' voices merge with traffic. They
are arguing. Their harsh words leave no mark
but fade into the dream of every day.
The clock goes ticking on but your life runs
straight down the hill of poetry and puns.

9

Most poetry runs down the hill of puns—
that is what makes it treacherous and yet
so utterly persuasive. Mothers and sons
can mumble ambiguities and let
that rich thick soup of meaning nourish them.
The language outside meets the ur-language within
with the consistency of dream
which sits like a faint moisture on the skin.
My father's voice. A gentle coaxing lost
in the depths of his chest. His musculature
is iron swelling in his arms. Thin frost
covers him in a Russian forest. Pure
narrative lines run through him. He stands
in the street with the city in his hands.

10

Out in the street, the city in his hands,
he crosses and recrosses, hard at work.
He builds his tongue of vowels and consonants
with ifs and buts, emerging from the murk
of winter. He gathers them up like notes
shuffled through the cold hands of the dead
who smile at us from under heavy coats
of dust and snow. The coins bear his own head
as guarantee. We're at a football match
above the river. The Brylcreemed players race
about the pitch in baggy shorts. We watch
the old men on the terraces. I see his face
darkening as we walk home. The light runs
along his arm which could be anyone's.

11

His arms and mine, both could be anyone's.
We're only bodies, bodies are what we have.
We float in them among the crowd in patterns
down the tidal street towards the grave
caverns of the tube. We are a small cell
in the organism which encloses us,
lost travellers, a tiny human smell
that thickens when we rise, like Lazarus,
spectral and intimate and normal, home
among the words that mean us and reflect
our faces and possessions. We are the Rome
that all roads lead to, the dense idiolect
of heavens where we sleep and wake. It stands
in the world, half Hungary's, half England's.

12

This tiny world, part Hungary, part England,
is the macaronic my parents speak—
my dad especially. There is no bland
unbroken stream. The words seem to leak
in drips, wearing away all sensible matter,
making minute impressions, exhausting them.
I see this and am lost in multicoloured chatter
that seems to spread and deepen: spit and phlegm
and croak and fricative whose sounds mean me
and everything that can be concentrated
into the me I vaguely sense, that free-
standing monument, marble and gold-plated,
sole owner of my lexical demesne
of spotless glass where words may sit and preen.

13

A spotless glass where anyone may preen
when it is dark outside, the window throws
your image back at you. Who is the unseen
and uninvited guest in your dumb shows?
Only the skin—hands, legs, face—remain
hanging against the house opposite. Hair
disappears, clothes vanish. And now the rain
jewels and fractures till you're hardly there.
Trying to say 'you' to those smears of light
seems inappropriate. Recall the face
of your mother, that hollowed out, tight
mask in the photograph, almost a grimace
in forty-five? It creeps under the screen
of language, blankly refuses to mean.

14

The language here blankly refuses to mean
what it's supposed to. The signs are lost.
If you could only read the space between
or babble in fiery tongues at Pentecost.
What's gone is gone. Parents might be the first
to vanish but children soon follow. The winter sun
flashes off snow and the icy trees burst
with light. The world is what cannot be undone
nor would you wish to undo it when it speaks
so eloquently out of its dumbness, when
its enormous treasury of hours and days and weeks
resolves to this sense of now and never again.
It comes at you now in syllabic storms,
the words withheld then loosed in angry swarms.

15

Words withheld. Words loosed in angry swarms,
screeching or singing till their meaning stales
have let you enter their strange world of forms
like faint vibrations down deserted rails.
Desire and loss do not permit debate:
articulate, you know how pain is drowned.
You slept in beds when day was never late,
your voice a channel for the kind of sound
that rolls downhill in poetry and puns.
Out in the street, the city in your hands
lays down its arms, which might be anyone's—
Hungary, England are verbal shadowlands
of spotless glass where all may sit and preen,
blank languages whose words refuse to mean.

Travel Book

for Anne Stevenson

1

The ego grinds and grates like a machine.
The voyage out begins in classrooms where
stout boys in dirty tracksuits measure clean
ruled sheets of paper to a helpless stare
which pierces the heart. The teacher croons
like a pigeon, her words a soft cloud
full of light. The boys' faces are balloons
that drift below her, a bobbing crowd
of stupid gentleness. This one smells of shoes
and mud. His fingers clench and unclench,
his hair a lank mess. He did not choose
his head or body. The beginnings of a stench.
His nose runs. His nails have been bitten
down to a tiny slip on which nothing can be written.

2

Look. On this tiny slip of paper is written
the name of a plain woman. The thick lens
of her heavy glasses seems to fatten
her eyelashes to strokes made by blunt pens.
Her name is *kindness* and *friendship* and *you
will never know*. Indeed, how could you know.
Later you watch her feeling her way through
her dusty hall. This is how the blind go
into the world, resenting its bulk, annoyed
by its ill manners, its crude mischief. To live
by touch reminds lovers of the void
between beauty and desire. Can she forgive
her dead husband, her visitors, all the unseen
nonsense her eyes feed on? What does it mean?

3

We feed on nonsense whatever it may mean.
A polished grand piano butterflies
across the room, billows across the clean
floor, over the stove which crackles and sighs,
and settles by the window. Dark brown gloss
covers the eyes of Mr Shane, violinist,
now worn quite smooth, his moustache a light moss
under his polished nose. His slender wrist
is almost feminine. Art has no gender,
is an uneasy comfort zone where the mad
briefly settle and the sane diminish in wonder
at their predicament, which is a sad
and brilliant obsession with pattern,
both raw and cooked, so soft and yet hard-bitten.

4

The self cooked through is soft and yet hard-bitten.
Two tiny flirtatious girls in the back room
of a photographer's flat seem to be wrapped in cotton-
wool. An air of sentimental gloom
haunts the refugee party. I touch the hand
of the elder one: the current lifts me from
my low seat. At nine, I cannot understand
what's going on. I know there is a bomb
ticking in her flesh. Years later I found out
her dad takes saucy pictures for calendars.
The younger one bursts into tears. There is a shout
in the street that rises above the growling of cars.
One understands that sex is nothing new.
The mirror is no censor but tells you who is who.

5

What does the mirror say to the censor? Who
else can you talk to? One good friend steals
your father's stamps. Another tells you
the secrets of his parents' bedroom. It feels
odd being in a world like this. You pretend
to be handsomer than you are. Jealous
of others' success you invent a girlfriend
who helps you develop your sense of the ridiculous.
Being what you are you value romance
above sex but cannot help your hormones.
You accompany your frail ego to the school dance.
The Christmas chill enters your bones
with a special, undisguised, personal tenderness
that creeps and cools, erasing self in the process.

6

Talk like this erases self in process.
But what is self? Here are the beauties of night:
Angela, deep voiced; white-socked Brenda; Diana, no less
dangerous; Carol delicate. All of them bite
with rejection. Rejection is the law
of late childhood. Now you should sing
the beautiful teachers who filled you with awe,
of whose lessons you remember nothing
but the transcendence of their look
as it fluttered here and there, who could not reject
because their job was not to. The text book
bears witness to their names. The high elect
drift in their cold empyrean, a vacant blue
out of your range, that seems both valid and true.

7

But how do you know what is valid or true
when there is no sense of being, no fixed space
to move in, no vantage point or overview?
You don't know if the world's a human place
or some robotic jamboree in which
you yourself must appear with appropriate mask.
Weakness is your only guide, that faint twitch
behind the eyes when you are moved to ask
the necessary question. Your father's eyes,
a fat woman struggling through the rain,
an awkward delicacy under the disguise
of the poised girl, that hard-to-explain
vulnerability of the big man, the lost distress
of the body in the mirror as it sees itself undress.

8

What do you see at night when you undress,
when the conscious mask slips between one breath
and another only to slip back on? A game of chess
played by some adolescent knight with a filmic Death?
The Bergmanesque Grim Reaper? The Old Foe?
The photograph of a youthful father? The flounce
of a dress your mother once wore? Under the slow
moment, the immediate, quick, once and once
only sense of transition. The shop-girl's shaking
hand as she pecks at the till. The brief smile
on the bus conductor's face as he is taking
your fare. Scrawled intercessions in the aisle
of the local church—those pregnant lines—
graffiti in the public toilets, signs.

9

Graffiti in the toilets, torn-down signs
at junctions. The Baptist minister glares
from his pulpit. Nearby, South Yorkshire mines
disgorge father and son. A teacher prepares
the next day's lesson. Peter Sutcliffe stalks
through Harehills and Chapeltown. In the pub,
girls in short leather skirts return from walks
down sidestreets, grab a spot of grub
and watch dominoes being slammed down hard
on marble tabletops. The whole world is
a dangerous romance, slowly edging forward
in the shadows, relying on memories
to get through its nightmares, meeting day
with the help of cigarettes, and cold pie on a tray.

10

Here is the ashtray's chaos, crumbs on a tray,
an empty glass. The blunt Northern accent
carries masculine warmth even in the grey
livery of garage and tenement.
Closed vowels, a rumbling in the belly.
Out on the moors harsher vowels of wind.
Spartan interiors. A sofa. The telly
by the wall. Down broken wet cobbles, blind
gropings of grass and weed. The poet in his chair
reciting Pope and Desnos. Children run
across a derelict site into a space that is nowhere
but must do. The city has room for everyone.
It does, after all, provide a kind of home:
crumbs on a tin tray, hair left in the comb.

11

Up-ended lead type, hair left in old combs:
lovers of small numbers go benignly potty;
big number men construct spectacular domes
and make long speeches. All is vanity
saith the preacher. A silver-headed man
labours among statues and word processors
turning language into an ingenious plan
to contain the universe and all its professors.
Why stop at the universe? My father picks
a stamp up with his tweezers and consults
his Stanley Gibbons. The world is full of maniacs
who hoard lost masterpieces in hidden vaults.
My mother vents her furies. The dictator resigns
after a fever, retires to a space between the lines.

12

After a fever, space between the lines
grows more attractive. Here the brittle hide
from gross events. A dazzling sun reclines
among the petals on the sill. Inside,
the cat pads across armchairs, a late fly
settles on the lampshade, the radio sings
to itself for ever and footsteps hurry by
without stopping. What continually brings
you up short? Your children trailing soft
fingers across the keyboard make their brief
excuses. Soon nothing substantial is left
except the words which offer no relief
from the bright precarious tedium of play
you read in negative at the end of the day.

13

You read in negative. At the end of the day
the light falls directly on you. Moon warms your skin
into endearments. My darling, you say
to the body whose pools you have swum in.
My dear. She catches a little moonlight
on her cheek and her shoulder. Now she dreams
of flying to her sick father, that shrunken, slight
figure in a distant bed. She moves through streams
of cloud and melts into sleep. The visitors
arrive with their negative gifts: the lamp
that glows black, cold fire, the open doors
of a closed room. It's hot in bed. She's damp
but cool—your life expands to fill the room
till there's nowhere to go. Come hope. Come home.

14

The question is where you go. Come hope, come home.
Her skin is palimpsest. You cannot read
her mind though you see it. At night, you roam
through the house watching the curtains bleed
to the floor. She is everything that holds
the pictures up, prevents headache, and turns
the world to language, sifting through the folds
of some larger brain, burning as fire burns
till you emerge like Tamino into music.
You try the word 'love', whisper 'death', and make
faces at yourself. You are growing sick
of eloquence. Perhaps you are beginning to awake
from the sleep of reason or are caught between
the teeth of words that grind like a machine.

15

The ego grinds and grates like a machine
producing tiny slips on which is written
the nonsense it feeds upon. What does it mean
to be a self, so soft and yet hard-bitten?
What does the mirror say to the censor? Who
talks like this, erasing self in the process?
How do you know if it's valid or true?
What do you see at night when you undress?
Graffiti in the public toilets, signs
in the ashtray's chaos, pie on a tray
of upended type, hair left in the comb
after a fever, the space between lines
you read in negative at the end of the day.
The question is where you go. Come hope. Come home.

Portrait of my Father in an English Landscape

for Peter Scupham

1

The classic shot of my father is the one
in which he carries my brother in his arms
with me striding beside him, holding on
to his trousers. The past continually warms
the present. The nostalgia gap
is a pit into which images can fall
and never rise. Best to suspect a trap.
Yet there is something solid and spherical
about the figure I feel I have to build
into and out of language. He exhales
his own monument which hangs there, stilled
as the light which holds him but fails
to preserve the cells of wind that whistle through him
and could destroy his body at a whim.

2

Easy to destroy a body. A historical whim
drops him into childhood among white beards
and piety. There he stands, forever slim
and vulnerable, entranced by old men's words.
He waits at the foot of the bed. Tales and jokes,
small beaky women. Parables and sweets.
How did Jesus get to be God? Women stroke
his dark hair. His grandmother always greets
the returning schoolboy with a small gâteau.
An uncle draws a bag of squashed éclairs
from his pocket. Outside, big winds blow
up a storm. The world of tables and chairs
will never know what hit it. Soon they are gone,
preserved elsewhere but not worth sitting on.

3

Preserves and cakes. Eventually time sits on
the lot. Grandad got run down by a tram
and yet survived to claim the insurance. One
uncle opened a music shop. It closed like a clam
about him. The second grandfather died,
cancerous, still telling stories. The little beaks
are pecking in the kitchen. They provide.
There was a brother once among the relics,
a home child, insignificant, a paradox,
who died when a hill of sand came down
and covered him as he was playing beside the rail tracks.
He had a name too, a genuine proper noun.
Short words. God's scattered text. The scholar's passim.
Even on clear nights certain stars look dim.

4

On clear winter nights when even the dim
stars interject splinters of blue ice
into the conversation, dead faces swim
through wisps of cloud. Dante's paradise
glows in bright rings around the moon. There is rank
and order in their passage. Or so they say.
Ghost stories, gothic tales. A hostile tank
rumbles across the city and levels the way
to disjunction. My father in the office.
My father in the factory. In the road
with a lavatory pan on his head. His surface
is a broken narrative. He must load
his possessions onto the conveyor belt
of particularities, hard luck and guilt.

5

Particularities, hard luck and guilt
compose him. Mention his patience too,
also his kindness. His eyes are a warm quilt
to hide beneath. You can wander through
his fingers as through a wood (though similes
are not his style). You see a short man
full in the chest, thin legs, large nosed. He sees
the likeness, suspecting metaphor, can
marshall facts, add a column of figures,
size up a problem and suggest solutions.
All fathers are Prospero or else beggars
without authority. There are fashions
in viziers as in haircuts. His alchemical head
radiates a thin light which must be interpreted.

6

By what light though can he be interpreted?
He is the history I stand on with one leg.
I'm trying to peer into the murk and shed
light on my own behalf. Must Prospero beg
for interpreters? Listen, he is playing
his mouth organ in the forest. Others hum
or search for words. Something is weighing
on them. The icy wind has made them numb.
Soldiers without insignia, dying slaves
out of Michelangelo, they learn the tunes
appropriate to their sad huts and lost enclaves.
Their families are telling fortunes
in safe houses and ghettoes others have built
into chains of command, their bones cracked, blood spilt.

7

Chains of command crack bones. The blood spilt
underwrites him. One day his friends stole
a supply train. A true tale on a single stilt,
another terrifying anecdote to roll
towards posterity. One of many. What hurts
is the truth of every story, things being just
as they are, true without consequence, bit parts
in a ridiculous epic of cinematic dust.
Escape on the March Back. The First Sight
of the Chaotic Russian Army as they Spin
across Half Europe, mad Flight, sane Flight,
the Toiling Masses, Rape, Rapine and Repin.
Malenky robot. Three soldiers in a bed,
the woman beneath them crippled, maybe dead.

8

A woman crippled if not exactly dead
(his wife, my mother) offers him her cage
and he walks in. He knows she has touched dread
with her bare fingers. There is a savage
untenanted domesticity I could not begin
to measure. The reader must devote
time to getting this right, develop a skin
too tender to feel the world as anecdote.
Time to detach oneself. An overweight
man with a hernia, bad short-term memory,
and need for companionship. Such late
revenges. Executions too summary.
I tell it wrong like he does. It's wrong to laugh
in the presence of a ghost or photograph.

9

The presences—not ghosts, nor photographs—
are symbols through which we walk together.
Our bodies are being resolved into epitaphs.
Outside, snow is working itself into a lather
about nothing. Language slips, words slide
and take pratfalls. I cannot quite conjure
this robust presence. Anecdotes hide
the very thing they describe in their pure
linear fashion. You can only focus
on one part of the picture, the rest shifts.
Perhaps that shifting is the true locus.
Perhaps anecdotes are frozen snowdrifts
that catch the light just so, shapes blown
and surfeited, whose centre remains unknown.

10

Surfeit of snow, the core remains unknown.
A winter park. He drags us forward, up
a slight hill. Our toboggan slithers on
and we descend. Soft landings. Now we cup
the snow in our gloved hands. A snowball.
The bus bonnet steams in the cold. The city
is an ice palace, the main street a great hall
approaching the square. His proximity
is his presence. The nearness of it. The wolf
enters his lair and asks for hot tea. The stove
in the corner warms us. Habitat and self
merge into sleep. It is a treasure trove
you cannot rob. The jewel's in the safe.
The wolf is in his lair. The children laugh.

11

The wolf in his lair, children begin to laugh
at their own fear. Kind wolf in a world of wolves.
Has father met the wolf? Wolves are the stuff
of legend. Their harsh morality revolves
about old prohibitions. One year dad fell
from the first storey of a building site. His green
face in the hospital bed was shrill as a bell.
Poor wolf in a world of traps. Again the clean
lines of anecdote. I remember how he stroked
my face. Not then. Some other time. Just once
he let fly at me, when he had been provoked.
I had upset my mother. I felt his palm bounce
off my cheek. This wolf bites. He stalks alone
down the high street. Old solitary. Dry bone.

12

The high street is full of loners. Dry bones
in shop doorways. Here comes the essences
under their layers of skin and flesh. Vague groans
of bodies in movement. Their circumstances
are apalling. We are not wolves but sheep
in the fold, gentle baas against the vast sky.
I imagine my father lying down, asleep
in that interior shelter where children cry
so faintly one can hardly tell their low
whimper from the dull sobbing of the wind.
The facts of any life are as they are, just so,
and never to be counted, stars in the sequinned
darkness, coloured sand to be sifted through
and banded, their edges neither straight nor true.

13

Bands of colour, edges just out of true,
conjure the Isle of Wight. I'm barely ten
and going through a religious phase. The blue
sky is the eye of God. Now and again
that clear sight homes in on something bright
and imposing. The teacher leads a prayer
like warm milk whose capillaries trickle right
down into my socks. No fatherly care
can ever be as sweet as this. The universe
has gentle hands to cradle a child's face.
It has its off-days too when it issues terse
directives, when it stares blankly at the place
relief should come from. I watch dad chew
his dinner, address him casually as you.

14

My father eats. I call him casually. You.
We argue for the sake of it as always,
because it is natural to argue.
I'm impatient. Some mischievous devil plays
us off against each other at opposite ends
of the table. I hate my impatience, hate
the cause of it. So hard to make amends,
impossible perhaps. It's getting late,
I look at my watch. He makes that worried gesture
with his hands which moves me. His eyes
are a warm cave swimming in faint moisture,
now turned inward, now open in surprise.
They hang there when the anecdotes are done.
The classic shot of my father. That's the one.

15

The classic shot of my father is one
easy to destroy. Historical whim
preserves a secret well worth sitting on,
though even on clear nights its stars are dim
particularities of luck and guilt.
He is a light that must be interpreted
through chains of command, cracked bones and blood spilt,
through women crippled, and often left for dead.
A presence, like the ghost in a photograph,
a surfeit, a core that can't be truly known.
The wolf is in his lair. The children laugh
in the high street at the old loner with his bone
and bandana, his edges neither straight nor true.
Their father waits for them and calls them You.

OXFORD POETS

Fleur Adcock

Moniza Alvi

Joseph Brodsky

Basil Bunting

Tessa Rose Chester

Daniela Crăsnaru

Greg Delanty

Michael Donaghy

Keith Douglas

D. J. Enright

Roy Fisher

Ida Affleck Graves

Ivor Gurney

David Harsent

Gwen Harwood

Anthony Hecht

Zbigniew Herbert

Tobias Hill

Thomas Kinsella

Brad Leithauser

Derek Mahon

Jamie McKendrick

Sean O'Brien

Alice Oswald

Peter Porter

Craig Raine

Zsuzsa Rakovszky

Christopher Reid

Stephen Romer

Eva Salzman

Carole Satyamurti

Peter Scupham

Jo Shapcott

Penelope Shuttle

Goran Simić

Anne Stevenson

George Szirtes

Grete Tartler

Edward Thomas

Charles Tomlinson

Marina Tsvetaeva

Chris Wallace-Crabbe

Hugo Williams